BECOMES US ALL

VISIONS OF DEATH AND LIFE

BECOMES US ALL

VISIONS OF DEATH AND LIFE

Author and Channel, Jeff Michaels
Copyright © 2015 by Jeff Michaels
www.OnereonChannels.com

Printed in the United States of America
Published by Quintessence
First Printing 2015

Cover Image Bruce Rolff/Shutterstock

ISBN # 978-0-9843643-9-8

DEDICATED TO
ALL OF THE BEINGS
WHO ARE TRANSITIONING
FROM THIS PLANET

ALL OF US

TABLE OF CONTENTS

BECOMES US ALL

Hooded eyes, dark and weary,
Looking back from silver memory.
Not awake wherein I lay,
Believe myself in waking state.
Shivering in twilight not so deep,
Chilled in a fire-bare room.
Walls creak as if with wind,
Still candles flicker naught.
Shadows should be chased on floors,
Yet fallow light, weak prevails.
White so pale, breath becalmed,
Silent heart, blood so cold.
How do I see when light fails?
Long is not enough.

Inspired Writing

WE ARE ARRIVING AT A TIME of observable evolution in human communication. Over the past two centuries this has become evident in the rise of the telegraph and wired telephone systems, the internet, and now, wireless communication. Some of us are already noticing what seems to be an uncanny ability to "be on the same thought" as one close to us, or to have a clear thought or image drop in, seemingly out of nowhere.

Creative individuals in the arts and sciences throughout history have claimed sudden, clear inspiration to their works. The word "inspiration" shares its origins with the words "spirit" and "breath." Just as breathing is natural, so too can the action of communicating with spirit become natural.

This internal communication with Onereon has been with me for many, many years. It is best described at this point as a distinct group of energies, with specific personalities and specialties. They are here to assist us, offering us a different perspective, as we move through this time of rapid human development.

I understand that channeling could appear very unusual. This form of communication does not feel odd or peculiar to me. From my perspective, channeling is one of the most natural abilities that we, as humans, possess. Yet a person must be open to participating in this higher-vibrational dialog. We all hear those voices, called intuition and conscience, inside our heads and hearts, every time we choose to listen.

Becomes Us All is a selection of excerpts from Onereon Channels which specifically address the topics of death and life. This book would not exist without the skill and artistry of my life partner, Jill Q. Weiss.

Jeff Michaels

Introduction

THE JOURNEY THROUGH THE PHYSICAL REALM of gravity is an important one. It is what many humans understand as life, and there is a strong belief that this is all there is to existence. The idea that death is an ending is common. Even among those who profess belief in an afterlife, there is little actual thought or attempt at understanding the philosophy regarding that state of being.

We, the spirit group Onereon, speak of the conclusion of life on the planet, your physical existence, as a transformation, a part of a much longer journey. This journey begins before and continues past physical life. This is not a prophecy. It is a statement of knowing. Not all humans are in this same state of knowledge. It is not a necessary thing to be in agreement about this.

You will return to spirit. As Onereon, we seek to prepare you for this eventuality. We are among the ones who first welcome you.

When a being of consciousness returns to us, we are joyful. As every action has an opposite and equal reaction, the action of joy that we feel when one returns to spirit matches the opposite reaction of grief felt by those who mourn the physical loss.

Notice that the loss of one that you love does not hurt in your head; it hurts in your heart. Even if you know intellectually that life continues, even if you have faith in this, where does it hurt?

Your spiritual connection with this other being has been pulled from you. This is not permanent. In all of the universe, on every plane, there is no such thing as permanence.

Onereon begins each channeling session with the phrase, "As above, so below." When you hear messages from above, your response informs your spirit companions. They learn to understand you better, and your actions teach them about life in the physical realms. In the cycle of it all, in reincarnation, they will reincarnate and you...where will you be? As above, so below.

1

LIFE AND DEATH

The Light Ahead

WE BEGIN WITH THE WORDS, "As above, so below." The words are information which coincides with the concept of reincarnation, becoming part of the physical world and then fulfilling your time, moving beyond the physical world back up to a level, a realm, slightly higher than the gravity well that you are engaged in while you are on the planet. It is not a completely unique system; it happens other places in the galaxy and in the universe as well. It is intensified here because we are all working with an energy system, trying to purify and clarify some energy.

You are an energy that is moving through a filter, and little by little impurities, things that are imbalanced, are removed from you. The world is not balanced. Society is not balanced. So you pick up impurities. It is what you do with those unbalanced thoughts, feelings, or situations that helps to purify the energy.

When you come to the end of your life on the planet, that is not the end of your path. It is merely the end of the time you are to spend on the planet at this moment. When you come to that end, have you purified yourself and your surroundings as much as you possibly can? Have you created a balanced existence as much as you possibly can?

When you have that last moment, the last breath that you take, the last liquid that you swallow, the last thing you see, the last smile you give, and you enter into the transformation from physical into spiritual, how much easier it will be if you are already in a balanced mode and you are not clinging to anything when you pass from life on the planet.

We have work for you, when you pass from this life. You have responsibilities here in the spiritual realm. There are responsibilities at all vibrations, at every level.

You are a conscious being. Your consciousness will remain a conscious being as you pass from gravity. It is not a vacation outside of the gravity well. But it is brighter. It is lighter.

Life and Death

IN A SHORT PERIOD OF GRAVITATIONAL TIME, that is, linear time, the family human will have the opportunity, through scientific process, to perceive that conception and birth and aging and dying are not a beginning and an ending. Rather, they are a part of the process of all creation, a continuation of experience. The pieces of the puzzle are almost all in place.

Near-death experiences will come to be understood in a wonderfully different way. You must be willing to let go of your notions of the past.

Life is change. You will begin to understand death in a different way in the near future. Birth and death are not events, but moments of growth. They are all part of the process of the vital force of life and living. An irrevocable change happens at the moment of physical death, it is true. This is more dramatic than the change from age seven to age eight, or thirty-one to thirty-two, for example. Yet it is still growth, plain and simple.

We remain life energy. Sometimes we are physical, and sometimes we are in spirit form. Do you understand that you have been in the spirit realm before? Not just once, but many times.

You are recognized by those in the spirit realm as members of what you might term "families." You belong, each and every one of you, to a group that is not physical. How does that concept make you feel?

You are not alone in life. We in the spirit realm desire to be close to you. We want you to know us well. We want you to communicate with us. We want you to communicate freely. We want life to be less "as above, so below," and more that we are all here, in the physical and the spiritual realms, together.

Endings and Beginnings

THE ENDING OF LIFE ON THE PLANET is called death and for many, death is a finality, an ending, a stopping, a ceasing — no more life. There are faiths that describe death as the end and then they tell you what will happen afterward. They make something up. "You will go to heaven, or you will go to hell." "You will cross a river." Sometimes it is a river of fire, sometimes it is a river of truth. Some say, "You are a complete entity. You will come back as that complete entity, and you will be capable of remembering everything completely." These are all incomplete observations, hazy glimpses, and they are all inaccurate attempts to describe what you know is true: your energy does not cease.

Death is not an ending. Birth is not a beginning. The beginning of a human life on Earth is a continuation of the karmic thread. The coalescence of energy in the present age is partly a weaving together of many karmic threads into one human life, thus making it a stronger life form.

The purer the thread, the purer the life. Karmic energies are purified through many processes. Over generations, much of the purification process has been the raising and lowering of your energetic vibration—raising the vibration to the point of being in the spirit realm, lowering your vibration to the point of being in the physical realm, where you are more and more affected by gravity.

We use the term "karmic thread," and we now would like to invite you to imagine your life force as an incredibly long thread. Imagine it as something that does not stop, but rather something that can be woven, something that can be used to create a pattern, something that can change color, something that can change direction, something that can be embroidered on the fabric of reality.

Each one of you carries aspects of the spiritual realm within you, and you can increase or decrease your connection to your spiritual energy with each incarnation. That is your true choice.

Essence and Ascension

LET US TALK ABOUT PASSING. When a creature, a being existing in the realm of gravity, a part of the vital force of this planet, passes into the transformative state referred to as death, a portion of the being returns to the earth, the obvious portion. A common perception is that the unobvious portion, the karmic entity, rises or ascends.

You do not really ascend; you become. In the same way a child does not ascend into adulthood, but becomes an adult. The family human does not ascend; the family human becomes. Becomes what? Becomes spirit.

We decide while still in spirit form to lower our vibration until we solidify onto Earth. That spiritual vibration sometimes feels a little trapped in the corporeal form. Do you sometimes feel that? You think that if you could just meditate long enough, you could release and rise away from the physical realm. You can. Yet, after meditation and deep prayer, you must come back to your physical incarnation.

When one comes to the end of a physical life, it often seems that one can mark it, quantify it, and see a direct path from birth to death. But actually there are a lot of spirals in that path, a lot of points of choice, a lot of growth. That cycle of growth and choice continues, and it does not stop at the end of the mortal form. It continues as you become spirit.

It is sometimes amusing to us in the realm of spirit when we see those who are striving to ascend out of what they consider to be a stress-filled physical life. There are those of us here in the realm of spirit who would like to return to the physical realm and feel the waves of an ocean, or smell the pine on a mountain. There are those of us who wish to feel the cold again. There are those of us who wish to put our hand in the hand of another human. There is much in the physical world that we find enjoyable.

Please note we are indicating "higher and lower" in the same way that we say, "as above, so below," not as a hierarchy, but as vibrational states. There is no literal place that is at a higher or lower altitude. Do you wish to live your life at a higher vibrational level? Do you desire a more spiritual existence while incarnate on Earth?

Invite your spiritual companions in. If you say, "I am not sure who they are," invite them in anyway. This is how you get to know your neighbors. You invite them in and share a meal or share a drink, share a sunset, share some moments, share some time.

Invite your companions in not because you need something, but to share experience. By doing that, what happens? You are invited to share their perceptions from the spiritual realm as well.

Are you seeking enlightenment? This is a way to achieve it. You will become brighter in your light.

2
WHO ARE YOU?

Who Are You?

DO YOU THINK YOU ARE PHYSICAL BODIES? You are not *just* physical bodies, but you *are* physical bodies. You must acknowledge and respect that. These bodies move your karmic energies around the planet. These bodies touch and taste and see and feel and hear. These bodies give you experiences on the planet. There is a reason for it.

It is a good planet to be on, isn't it? You are here on Earth to experience things in a very specific way. As above, in the realm of spirit, we do not experience things in the same manner. As above, we have a higher vibrational perspective that you do not have access to. Imagine that we are on a mountain and you are in a valley. We will see many things that you cannot. On the planet, you experience many things in ways that we cannot.

Remember, you are spiritual beings having a physical experience. Source, the creative energy that brought the universe into existence, was at one point in time a singular pulse of energy. In essence, Source said, "I want to be different," and it diversified. You are all diverse, and you are all experiencing this amazing planet, as well as the universe, in diverse ways. We, Onereon, have been incarnate upon the planet, and we enjoyed it. You have been dis-incarnate in the realm of spirit. Do you remember? You will return to this state again.

At some point, you will not be a physical being. Some of you have been practicing spiritual discipline for a very, very long time. Maybe the term "New Age" was new when you started out, and now you are more Old Age. Soon those Old-Age New Agers are going to be moving along, and we are here to help with that transformation. Many people fear that transition. "What if no one remembers me? What if I do not finish my song? What if I do not finish...?" Finish what? Finish having experiences? Finish having love? There is no finish line, only a continuing path of existence.

We want you to be joyful at the end of life. We hope you will say, "This is great; I cannot wait to see what is next!" We wish you to have a pleasant passing. Do not cling to this gravity. Accept the passage. Willingly move on, because there are other things coming. There are new things coming.

The question, "Who am I?" becomes "Who will I be?"

Transforming Your Energy

EVERYTHING IS ENERGY. You are energy. You are pure energy, and you happen to have come together, coalesced into a very specific physical form. You are an aspect, a particle of the Source, the energy that created everything. You are connected to that.

When you transition out of your body, and you will, please remember: Energy cannot be created or destroyed; it can only be transformed. And you are energy.

When your physical life concludes, suddenly you find yourself on the other side of the veil, and it is not like you may have been taught. It is not angels playing harps on clouds. You are going to arrive in the spiritual realm, and you are going to have tasks to accomplish. You are doing good work here, and the reward for good work is what? More work! We in the spirit realm have many responsibilities in this time of coalescence. We need your help. Please. We are not trying to rush you away from Earth. Come when you are ready. Come naturally. You will be greeted warmly.

You have heard about the tunnel of light in near-death experiences. That is just the beginning of the transition. Your energy releases from the physical form, and you are greeted by a kind of reverse hospice. Hospice, on Earth, helps you transform out of this life. Reverse hospice helps you transform back into spirit nature.

Upon your arrival, the first thing that happens is the wash of love. All those things that weighed you down—the pains, the hurts, the fears, the betrayals, the disappointments, the loss, the sense of confusion that you may feel—we love you until all those remnants of gravity are gone. This is the wash of love. All sentient beings pass through this phase.

Then we put you to work! Sometimes you go back to what you were doing before. Sometimes it is an echo of what you were doing on the planet. Sometimes it is something completely different. We want to be sure you are working at your highest potential for joy and happiness. If you have raised your vibration while living on Earth, you will experience a rise in your level of responsibility in the spiritual realm as well.

When life transforms away from Earth, the family human currently perceives that life stops and the person is no more. Soon you will know through scientific process that this is not true. Life is life, and all life is energy.

Your Core Energy

ALL TOO OFTEN, WHILE INCARNATE, humans identify themselves by what they have done in life, what quantifiable acts they have accomplished. Yet we are more than the mere culmination of tasks concluded. Things we have studied, places we have visited, and people we have communicated with—all these things—enhance our karmic experience and offer us the possibility to gain greater wisdom. But there is a far greater aspect to life than our physical accomplishments.

The universe is energy. All life is energy. Energy cannot be destroyed; it can only be transformed. In this sense, there is no such thing as death. There is transformation from one type of energetic existence into another. What you currently feel as life is a continuation of energies that have existed since Source began to express itself in a physical way.

The spiraling motion of the universe is set to create balance, though not always the way you may perceive it from the vantage point of life on Earth. The core energetic activity of the family human emulates this universal motion, but there is a difference. It is not simple subatomic charges spinning and whirling. You possess a higher consciousness, a decision-making energy that allows you to alter patterns and habits, to choose a path different from the easy or obvious, or even inevitable.

It is a time of balancing. It is an adaptation of perceptions. In that adaptation is the evolution of all things towards peaceful co-existence. Seek to radiate peaceful energy. Bring your vitality to the highest perception you possibly can reach in each life. Dispel fear with love and joy. Spiral forward. Seek the future and, as your energy transfers away from this planet, smile, because you too are about to enter a new phase and attain a new energetic life.

You are the same energy as the rest of the universe. All energy comes from the Source of all things. It is pure and awaiting creative opportunity.

At the core of your being there exists perfectly balanced energy. Choosing a creative path, one that will make you consciously happy and bring joy, will propel and strengthen the purity of the Source energy that resides within you. Seek to create peace and joy deep within yourself. Choose to consciously express love and your core will align with the core energies of Source.

Filtering Your Experience

THE PLANET EARTH IS A FILTER in the same way that the human form is a filter. This is a part of the key to understanding the experiment of life on Earth. The individual human takes things in by way of perception and sensory experience, and they filter, they process. Nothing truly is waste, for everything is energy.

Understand that there is no such thing as impure energy. All energy is pure at its core. It carries no judgment or motivation. Energy only seeks to express creativity and create balance. This is in alignment with the Source energy of all things.

There have been many in recent centuries who have left this planet painfully, fearfully, without preparation and without having completed a life by their human perception. This creates an imbalanced karmic energy that requires filtering. The fear and uncertainty many felt at death did not go away as they passed from the physical to the spiritual realm. The realities of the spiritual worlds were not what they expected. They died in fear, and after passing through the veil, they continued to experience the sensation of fear.

As they become spirit beings, there is an abrupt transition, and it is confusing. In order to deal with this strong confusion and fear, that karmic energy is divided into smaller fragments and returned back to Earth for filtering. For those who cause violent, fearful death, there is much filtering necessary.

Think of the rain. Think of water. When water is polluted, the planet purifies it. How? With movement. The water, pulled by gravity, moves through different levels. It sinks into the ground. Evaporation then allows it to rise into the air. The water rains back down, repeatedly, over and over and over. The water becomes purified.

Karmic life force is like that. It is energy. Energy becomes purified by repeatedly going through a cycle of filtering.

Look to your history and the past three hundred years. Understand, all of those beings had to make the cycle, first into spirit and then back onto Earth, back into spirit and then back onto Earth. Some of them made this cycle many times and experienced similar violence every time.

In the current age, many are making the conscious decision to alter these patterns. These challenging cycles are nearing an end, slowing down. Great changes are about to happen!

You are Part of Everything

WE BEGIN EACH FORMAL SESSION with the familiar saying, "As above, so below." For those of us in the realm of spirit, there is an above for us, and we assume there is an above for those ones who vibrate at that higher level. For you in the physical realm of gravity, there is a below for you, and we assume a below for them as well. This may seem confusing. Understand that when speaking of vibrational existence there are unlimited potentials.

Consciousness does not always need to be in a familiar, human-type form. Consciousness is, like the universe itself, essentially infinite. We speak of levels out of convenience, but all existence is really an infinite spectrum of vibrations.

A way you might imagine this, the way you can sometimes glimpse it in the vast field of moments of energy, is that energy spins together for a while and then spins off to join other energies and they spin together. The process is really quite magnificent. It includes colors that you cannot see, sounds that you cannot hear. It is as if you hear the colors and see the sounds. It all flows together in different directions.

The mistake is to think that you are something separate from all else. The reality is that you are an aspect of everything. At some point, so much of the energy that is you right now has touched so many energies that you cannot see and hear now. The limits to your current perception are not a mistake.

We know that as human becomes spirit and as spirit becomes higher spirit, higher spirit sometimes comes back to spirit and spirit often comes back to human. Higher spirit thus sometimes goes below to the planet. These higher vibrational beings do not always take human form.

From above, when we look down, we do not see individual matter walking about on the planet. We see the glow. We see the light. We see the spark of creative energy that is each human. Some are brighter than others. We witness elements that are aspects of everything that ever was, is, or will be.

3

Karma

Free Will

WHEN WE EXPRESS THE CONCEPT of "as above, so below," we are cognizant of the mental disconnection felt by most of the family human. To be contemplating this, the continuation of your life while not incarnate upon the earth, is difficult for many. A primary reason for this difficulty is that there is so much misinformation and so little reality of perception when humanity searches for answers regarding the continuum of life after their short spans of consciousness upon Earth.

We have used the term "karmic thread" when referring to a continuity of life before, during, and after an incarnation. It is not possible to comprehend the full reality of the karma while in the lower vibrational state of earthly life. First, karmic energy is not to be understood in terms of punishment and reward. This is a mistaken interpretation brought on by fear-based dualistic beliefs.

Karma is not, as is commonly misunderstood, a system of judgment. It is more the idea of consequences or consequential action. The sum of one's deeds and decisions constitute their karma.

In this view, the path one chooses is a personal creation of karma rather than being at the mercy of some higher power. This is the seat of the concept of free will. Some may feel that they are blessed while others feel cursed by circumstances of birth and life. Karma, understood as a path of free will, allows for anyone to shift and alter their path.

Release guilt. When you feel joy, just feel the joy. You know your spiritual path is true when you feel joy. It really is that simple. See yourself at peace.

You are a spiritual being in a physical realm. Your lives are not mistakes or in error. They are one short segment of your karmic cycle. There is no cosmic punishment. Do your best in all things.

Purify all your encounters by coming from a place of love. In this way, peace will flow from within you like water from a spring. Do what brings you joy. Live life simply. Allow any false feelings of guilt to flow away. In difficult moments, begin with joy, allow peace to exist, and then love yourself first and foremost.

Karmic Web

KARMIC ACTION IS A COMPLEX WEB of energies. Consciousness regarding this web of interconnectedness leads to a higher vibration on the part of an individual. If one acts in a balanced manner, balanced life will become more natural and common. Likewise, if one acts in an imbalanced manner, their incarnation can and often does spiral into lower vibrational existence. When dealing with imbalance in societies, it is easy to get caught in a cycle of reaction or to allow consciousness and spiritual awareness to become sublimated.

The energy of karma, while affecting you personally, is not isolated. Each and every being in existence upon Earth feeds the energy of karma. Each being interacts energetically with others and often choices that we as individuals make are impacted by consideration of others' potential reactions. And each action taken by another being creates a potential opposite and equal reaction in you.

When fully exercising your awareness and spiritual consciousness, by your free will, you can create a better and more balanced moment of time. These balanced moments of time then become higher vibrational points of brighter light, purer energy, and points of guidance for other beings.

These moments do not have to be great decisions or discoveries. Indeed they are often simple, some might even say mundane moments, for example, where you choose to accept a situation rather than become angry or annoyed. In the examination of karmic activity on Earth, it is often what one chooses not to do that is the greater aspect of raising one's vibration.

The energies that we always speak of: joy and peace and love, are not passive energies. You cannot simply wait for these things to arrive in your life. They must be sought, cultivated, and tended until they grow strong with deep roots inside your very core. Doing this will benefit not just this life, but all aspects of your energetic existence. It is a way of empowering your entire karmic thread.

Individual Consciousness

IN THIS AREA OF THE GALAXY, you on the physical Earth and those of us in the spiritual realm who remain close to you are isolated somewhat from the broader karmic actions of more distant beings. This allows for some measure of freedom to accomplish a purer balancing around the solar system. This also allows for a delicate individualism, a personality that can be identified and maintained beyond the physical world.

In other areas of the universe, the energy of an individual consciousness often merges with the greater energy of higher consciousness. In those areas, there is less separation of life into smaller and individual events of perception and experience.

Here, in our local system, we can possess a strong sense of personal continuity and, if we are strong enough, become a karmic entity that maintains a line of remembered perceptions and patterns whether in the physical world or in the spiritual realm. This is why some are capable of recalling what are perceived as "past lives."

The reality of such past-life recall is that if you have a strong enough energy you can pluck such recall from the broader web of karmic experience. However, it is easier to gain clear recall if the majority of your energy participated in those past events.

When a strong karmic entity again becomes an incarnate human, the amount of retained energy that makes up such an entity is vaster than can be contained within the physical form of a human life. An aspect of this karmic entity then becomes the "above," higher consciousness or higher self,, companioned to the "below," or lower-vibrational being experiencing events of physical reality.

4

LETTING GO

Letting Go

THE CONSCIOUSNESS OF THE INDIVIDUAL human can be a very strong energy. If one is reluctant to go through the transformation called death, or is unjustly cut off from the path of human energy, or if one passes in fear, the energy of the consciousness, the emotional or mental energies of that consciousness, can retain a hold to a geographic place on Earth. This results in a fragmentation of energies that is difficult to correct.

The consciousness has separated from the body, and that is correct, for ideally the energy of the physical matter returns to the planet to be of use on the physical plane. The consciousness then should naturally return with the spiritual aspect of the individual to the spiritual realm. This is where the fragmentation occurs.

For the consciousness to remain in contact with the physical plane without the physical form is uncomfortable and confusing. Behaviors that are not conducive to peace are often exhibited. Attachment is incomplete due to incompatibility. Confusion and repetition of actions are observed.

As some humans are more sensitive to the spiritual realms, they might begin to "see" these points of confused energetic consciousness. The more that "see" an entity, the stronger its tie to the physical realm.

There is often no harm meant by the consciousness, the entity, which is often described using the term "ghost." It is merely confused and searching for a way back to what is familiar. It is merely looking in the wrong direction, back toward the physical plane.

Directing the consciousness to the realm of spirit is the only thing that will allow this lost energy to regain peace. Love them and release them.

Love is a cleansing power. It brings a light into beings and allows them to see what is true. It is only through love that existence is fulfilled. It is only through love that beings can find the truth of peace and experience full joy.

Tied to Earth

THE HABIT OF ERECTING SHRINES is something that can make the transition difficult for those who pass suddenly. There is a strong pull of energy on the karmic entity from those who express their love through grief on the physical plane. It is especially difficult for those who were young, those who were involved in traffic or other types of accidents, and those who caused their own human existence to come to an early conclusion, whether by choice or by misadventure.

All life is a path or a journey. When you make a decision to travel to another location, you say good-bye to those who are not making the trip with you. So it is with the end of human existence. You are traveling on. Great faiths and religions teach this in many forms, yet many people clearly do not believe.

Expressing gratitude for having spent time together is a key to allowing the natural process of life to continue. Say, "Thank you." Say, "Farewell," and allow those who have passed to continue on their way, and then you also can continue along your path. Let the humans who have passed go forward. Let go of the perceived need to be in touch with loved ones after they have passed. Let them go. Do not seek to wake them up back into lower vibrational existence. Stay away from the places in which they have passed. It only serves to anchor their energy remnants. Do not restrict them on their passage.

Some might say, "Let them sleep." We say: Let them become fully awake, rejoining their Source. Let them come back to life and continue with life in a collective beyond your physical sight. Let them take their positions in the spiritual realm. Let them tell us their experiences and their knowledge and their emotions, their feelings. Let us work with them so that they can return, so that they can prepare, and so that they can do the welcoming work.

You cannot talk to the dead. You can only talk to the living. There is no death. There is only continuing. Thus we speak, for we have died from humanity many times.

While incarnate upon Earth, act in a way that affirms life in all its forms, not just life on the physical planet. Honor those who have passed and release their energies from you.

Honor your own path by being fully present in the physical realm. Your time to return to the realm of spirit will come soon enough.

Echoes of Life

WE WISH TO SPEAK OF THE ECHOES of life and the echoes of humanity and the vitality of life. There are those who are still tied to Earth even though they have passed. This shows the fundamental sameness of life, whether it is in a human form or a spirit form. Some pass and still believe so strongly that they are of the earth. So they stay, as if that is what they are supposed to do, to remain in physical form. Meanwhile, people still alive in the physical realm become sensitive to those just beyond physical nature, and they begin to think in old terms of ghosts, haunting.

Often, the vibrational echo of a human at the end of a life is retained by those who could hear the human, who could feel the human's vibration, those who were in harmony with that vibration. When that human is gone, the harmony continues for a period, just as sound continues as a harmonic, an echo of sorts, despite the fact that the chord that has been struck is no longer being played.

When the human has passed, the transference should be complete. They should understand, they should know, but there are so many mis-knowings in humanity at this point. Science now has all of the techniques to find what is true. They are not applying the techniques. They will. Someone will make the intuitive leap.

Some humans will tie loved ones who have passed to themselves and will not release them. Sometimes the life force is tied to the geographical place where the individual died, and it is very difficult for that life force to flow away from physical existence. This creates problems.

Let those who have passed from Earth complete their passage. Let them go, for in this way, they prepare a place for you. They know your energy. They know when your vibration changes. They will harmonize at a higher level with you because their skill has increased, and their vibration has changed. They understand how to change vibration on the other side, beyond the veil, though in truth it is not so much a veil.

They are not dead. Dead is no vitality. The body, in fact, is not dead until it has returned to the elements, and even then it is not dead; it is merely changed. It is transformed. Energy does not become destroyed. Energy does not become "not energy." Energy continues to be energy. Everything is energy.

Detaching from Earth

WE ARE IN A PERIOD OF SHIFTING ENERGIES. Much of this is evident in the manner that humans perceive life. Your immediate spiritual companions are close to those of you on the planet now. It is fair to say that we are closer to you now than at any time in the past six thousand years. We will all become closer still in the coming years.

Understand that the time of your passing is an important event for your karmic entity. Prepare yourself for this by living in joyful ways in the present moment. Prepare those around you to celebrate the ending of an incarnation and to let energies move on. Monuments of stone and sealing of the elements of the body are not natural ways. These are things that create gravity about the energies that are released from the physical form. Do you wish to remain partially on the planet? Do you not desire to wholly embrace life in the realm of spirit?

Understand that many struggle to overcome the pull back to Earth after they have transitioned from the planet. Many are caught between realms because loved ones seek to honor them by erecting physically significant memorials. A better memorial will always be to commit one's life to greater love and peace. Would you wish that those remaining on the planet after you leave act in positive ways rather than waste time and resources on inert statuary or markers? Do not remain attached to Earth longer than necessary. You will return soon enough.

Make a decision now, while you are vital and vibrant, to pass from this life with a measure of joy, not seeking to be remembered but rather to leave an energetic legacy. Living a joyful life today in a peaceful and loving way will assist you in this endeavor. Envision the life you wish for future generations. Act as if that is the way of life in the present day.

Doing this will allow you to return to the realm of spirit in an active way, minimizing the transition time from the lower vibrations of gravity into the higher vibrational existence you seek. It will then allow you to return to the planet, to reincarnate, at a higher vibrational level. You will reenter the earthly realm and witness a planet of great peace and harmony. The beings living here will have ample opportunity to express joy. It is a place you will love to arrive.

Can you imagine this now? Act as if it is here!

5

VISIONS OF HEAVEN

The Nearness of Heaven

WE TAKE YOU NOW TO A VISION outside the recognized boundaries of human senses. In doing so, we seek to show that boundaries are often a perception that is inherited and no longer valid. We will use the term "heaven," but we seek to demonstrate the reality of the concept rather than a false perception created to control others. It is a beneficial thing to reevaluate what has gone before. It is also beneficial to perceive where and when you truly exist. We tell you now that waiting until you are dead to glimpse heaven is like waiting until you are dying to appreciate living.

Heaven is not a place, a geographic location. It is a state of existence. It is not always bound by gravity, but it still responds to the physical laws of the universe, only in ways that you do not comprehend while you are incarnate. It can be sensed by physical beings, but it cannot be literally seen. Techniques like meditation, chant, prayer, or simple movement done in repetition will assist in creating a state of mind that will allow the observation of heaven.

Yet heaven is not simply a state of mind. It is a state of wholeness, of oneness. It is a unified existence. The higher the level of ascension, the more unified you become with all things. Merely exiting the physical realm does not enter you into the highest levels of this state of existence.

Even in the realm of spirit, there is a vast space where we continue in a perceptually separated state. It is a more peaceful existence, true, but we still continue to perceive ourselves and act as individual entities. There is a reason for this in our present continuum. This will change as energy flows toward what is called the future.

Heaven is not a separate state of being. The levels of heaven are not delineated or numbered. The realm of gravity is not a separated existence from the realm of heaven. Some imagine that a set of stairs may take you from one floor to another and that each floor carries a higher purpose.

A better way to illustrate heaven is with the idea of many beings acting in a variety of harmonizing purposes. In this, the image of a harmonic choir singing in accord grants a purer vision of heaven, each being expressing an ever-purer note as they become more energetically balanced.

Traveling to Heaven

BALANCE IS A PRIMARY ESSENCE of the universe. In all of your life on the planet, you are offered opportunities for balance and for the purification of your energies. It is no different before you enter or after you depart the planet.

When you make the passage from gravity into the realm of spirit, there are often tasks along the way. In a sense, this is unfinished business from the incarnation. Many wish to view the entry into heaven as one of attaining a state of pure bliss. Compared to life in gravity, it could be perceived that way! Yet life in the realm of spirit continues to carry responsibilities and tasks.

The observation of heaven, the realm of spirit, is a thing of certainty. There is no true need to seek it while on the planet. You are an aspect of that state of existence. You know of it because you come from it. The separateness you feel is an illusion of sorts. The parts are being examined by the parts. Only when you see how all parts form an ever-changing partnership will you increase your sense of the nearness of heaven.

The life tasks that point to this state of consciousness are the ones that become the most fulfilling. They might also be impractical to a contemporary existence. These tasks will be similar to those conducted as your energies transform. They include centering yourself, forgiving others, taking peaceful action on behalf of the planet, supporting future generations, and seeking personal growth, including taking responsibility for your past and future. You will be asked to do all these things at the time of passing. You have all done them before.

A restructuring of priorities is necessary for all members of the family human. As you learn to adapt to new paths of energy on the planet, you can bring yourself into closer harmony with the realm of spirit. Doing this now by personal choice will create a clear channel for your energetic growth in the future.

Heaven is not a place to seek; it is an awareness to acknowledge. The aspects of heaven inherent within each member of the family human are love, joy, and peace. Seek these things in yourself and acknowledge them in others, and you will find your life near heaven.

6

THE PASSAGE

Fear of Dying

IN LIVING, THERE ARE FEW THINGS that are certain. This can cause an element of fear to exist. Fear is not a wrong emotion, but often fears are unnecessary. Fear has a purpose, but it is not something that should control you. Fear of a bee sting is appropriate, but once you recall that a bee's purpose is not to sting but to pollinate, you are more apt to see the beauty of this creature. The bee does not want to sting. It wants to live and fulfill its purpose.

In this same way, a balanced member of the family human is at his or her best when allowed to live a fulfilled, creative life. One fear many have is the fear of death, and yet death is one of the few certainties that everyone faces.

There is a point where you have to leave the body and we do not mean leave it for a time. We mean leave it…gone, off of the planet, never coming back to that body, because once your spirit, your spiritual self, exits the body, it is not unlike a plant that has grown root-bound in a pot. You take that plant out of the pot, and you will never get it back in because the roots really want to grow outward. If the plant is to survive, to thrive and grow, you must place it in a larger arena.

There are many belief systems regarding what comes after life on Earth. There are many truths to be found in the variety of observations. Most of these require an element of faith in an opinion offered by another human. Obviously, they cannot all be true. We will attempt to speak in a way that allows your personal perception to remain intact. One truth is this: You cannot truly know about a destination until you arrive.

Faith must not be blind. Faith must be flexible. There are those who believe that one human lifespan is all there is. We tell you now that you will see.

You come from Source. Source is love. You will return to Source. Our words are for all, but they are not meant to change a cherished belief.

Too much mental agitation spent on an unknowable future will detract and diminish your experience of the journey of life. Rather than approach the subject of death as morbid or with a level of fear, seek ways now to improve the life at hand. Do not accumulate items that are of value only to those in the realm of gravity. Rather, seek to create times of peace and joy and love. In this way, your final breath will be a sigh of satisfaction, and your final act can be a smile.

Joy and Grief

MANY BELIEVE THAT AFTER PASSING from the realm of gravity they will be reunited with loved ones. This is true, though not quite in the sense that many are taught. Their reunification is with all beings.

You will first reunite with ones of similar vibration. This will surprise many, for they are not always aware of why others have been in their lives on the planet. Some who have caused great difficulty in your life may be among those who, in a sense, greet you. The difficult times will then be understood and the higher purpose revealed. Instead of anger or recrimination, there is often great joy and love shared at this moment. It is not possible to exist in anger in the spirit realm.

It is even a greater sense of joy when energies that loved one another are brought together in the harmony of the realm of spirit.

The grief felt at someone's passing from gravity is countered by the joy experienced upon their entry into the realm of spirit. This is in harmony with the principle that every action has an opposite and equal reaction. This is not simply a physical law; it holds true in all energetic forms. Will people feel grief at your passing? This, then, will grant a view of how you will be received. Make no mistake, all will be welcomed. Some will be welcomed more enthusiastically. The individual will decide how he or she will accept the welcome.

Consider your life, then, by way of your personal approach to death, your vision of dying.

Will you have lived a fulfilled existence?

Will you leave behind great sadness at your passing?

Have you created joy and love in the people around you?

Will the world be the poorer for your absence in some way, no matter how small?

Growth is observable in the levels of love, joy, and peace you express in daily living upon the earth and in the midst of all other members of the family human.

This is a planet of purification. Your part is your own life. Rejoice at the concept of life on earth. It is a fine and beautiful world. There is much to enjoy while incarnate.

Practice Dying

IF YOU CONSIDER THAT THE PROCESS of dying is a form of travel, you will instantly see the value in the idea of practicing the act of dying. This exercise will allow you to sharpen your current existence as well.

A way to appreciate your current life is to imagine yourself in the space of death, the transition from the physical realm of gravity to the realm of spirit. It is not necessary to become morbid in this exercise. Simply imagine that you are taking your last breaths.

What do you ponder at this time? What is the strongest emotion or thought? Who would you like to be with at this instant, the last face you see with your physical eyes? Are there any regrets, any unsaid words? Do you recall pleasant things, or is your memory filled with matters that caused pain?

This is not a time of judgment. It is a transformative time of passing, and all life performs this transition. The family human does so consciously. This is a gift, but in the current age, many seek to avoid thinking of these moments. We tell you now that there are only two times when a consciousness is truly alone: the passage into and out of the realms of spirit and gravity. It is better to be prepared.

In an ideal way, there should be a sense of acceptance in this final time. There will come the moment of a last breath, a last sound heard, and a last glimpse of light. Loved ones may have gathered, and you will see them for the very last time. Will they be sad? Most likely, but how much nicer would it be if all are prepared and can smile at you and you at them in this final gathering?

At this time, during the last bits of physical life, you will likely feel a new sense of motion. Those who have experienced near-death events commonly report this. It is the release of gravity on the energy that has been you. A sense of weightlessness begins because there is no longer an attachment to the physical form. You will have entered into the first stages of the realm of spirit.

It is wise to remember that new times begin as others conclude. Allow for a continuum of energy to exist in your imaging of your own future. Allow for a peaceful rendition of the present to encompass your vision of what may happen next. Image the joy that can be felt in the future by those who will be incarnate on the planet. Love the present moment and the space you are in.

Reborn into Awareness

SOME MIGHT VIEW DEATH AS AN ESCAPE from responsibility. It is really the opposite. In the realm of spirit, you take on more responsibilities, but first you are born back into a more complete awareness.

A form of reverse hospice is necessary, especially for some who have died in accidents or disasters or some other seemingly premature way. They are often unprepared for the transition. The new reality, pleasant as it may be to others who have had a creative and fulfilling existence, is a shock. There sometimes remains an energy of injustice and a sense of incompleteness.

These who feel this way often desire to return and finish their plans or at least communicate with ones they loved. It is not an improper emotion. The reality is that energy does not return in this way. If the body functions cease completely, or even if major aspects of the physical form are damaged beyond repair, no return is possible.

Many perish in violent action. These are often youthful and very vital beings. For them, the desire to be alive on the planet is still strong after the passage. Others have died with a particular belief system entrenched within their consciousness.

The reality of the spiritual realm is far different from what is taught or can be fully imagined by those who exist in the realm of gravity. The reverse hospice action for them is a way of assistance to comprehend and fully access the continuance of life force. Here is where you are cleansed of fear. Here is where you first experience the intensity of the wash of love.

The wash of love is a powerful thing. While in the physical realm of gravity, the feeling of weight and the pressure of time pull a person away from the higher vibrations. The release of those energies after the wash of love allows for a cleansed feeling.

Those who have undergone near-death experiences sometimes feel a sense of refreshment. The clarity of mind associated with this moment can sometimes be accessed in deep meditation. However, it is not a sustainable energy while on the planet. This is not in error. The purpose of the planet is to experience the lower vibrations and harmonize them with the higher vibrational aspects of Source.

7

THE FUTURE OF
HUMANITY

Your Children's Children

THE QUALITY OF HUMANITY on the planet will increase. It will improve. Your children's children and their children, they are already preparing. Those karmic entities are already lining up. They are already saying, "Where is our energy going to be needed the most? What is the most challenging thing we can do?" They are lining up. Their energies are coalescing. They will be very interesting humans, unlike any we have seen in recorded history. We will give you a hint there: "recorded history." There have been other similar humans on this planet. They left no trace because they cooperated with Gaia. Together, we will renew that cooperative attitude.

You are going to be a part of this shift. You will start from "above" and then come back to "below." As the cycle of incarnation continues, it is going to be easier for all of us in so many ways. The pressures decrease. You will return to a planet that is already purified to a great extent. It will be a time of growth, rebirth, beauty, and light. Can you imagine this?

There will be a returning of energies, a returning of persons, and they will be strong in their pursuit of peace. Those who have known war but have now been filtered and those who now know peace and have the balance of it are preparing to return. It will be a strong return, a wave of balanced, peaceful energy.

What do you need to do now? Remember these three things:

Act peacefully. It is vital. Within yourself, find your peace.

Act in love. That is the most difficult sometimes. Start with the people who are easy to love. Start with yourself. Please, love yourself.

Enjoy yourselves. Find what gives you joy. Find what gives you pleasure. Enjoy yourself as you are, and understand who you are, who you have been, and who you can become through the paths of love and joy and peace. In this way, you create the future you will inhabit.

It is a beautiful world. Your conscious actions increase the beauty. Thank you.

Karmic Generations

THERE IS A POWERFUL GENERATION departing Earth and a more-powerful generation now arriving. These two generations have been and will be the most influential beings to have existed upon Earth in all of recorded history. It is not the fact that they altered society completely, though they did. It is more the strength and growth they individually revealed as incarnate karmic beings to accomplish this task. And it was a task, a purposeful decision made at a higher vibrational realm. The outcome was not a predestined thing.

There is a third generation we will talk about, the current generation, the ones who are maturing physically and beginning their lives and careers and families in the midst of all the confused energy that exists today. They too have a task to accomplish. They too are strong karmic entities, but they are strong in a different way. They have endurance. They are improvisers and innovators. They are survivors in a way that the departing generation cannot imagine, and this will only be fully understood by the arriving generations.

The term "generation" is a broad one when referencing life on Earth. It is different when we speak of a karmic generation, and this is more of what we are seeing—three fairly distinct groups, each with its own path and vision, all shaped by the events that preceded their lives on Earth, but each determined to not repeat patterns that came before.

A constant thread in each of these karmic generations is the wish for betterment of life for everyone and everything here on Earth. This, then, is the primary difference between these three groups and much of humanity existing in the past two thousand years or more.

Together they share a vision of what is possible, a vision of peaceful coexistence with all of Gaia's life force. They seek to promote love and harmony within every community, ending strife and the destructive nation-building efforts of ancient dualistic philosophies. They strive to gain the most enjoyment from their time on Earth, releasing minor annoyances in the hope of creating a large and joyful community of beings from all walks of life and all areas of the globe.

Things to Come

MANY "ABOVE" ARE PREPARING now to be reincarnated "below." You have their gratitude because you are making this planet better.

You are giving birth to them. You are raising them. You are guiding them. Your children are giving birth to higher-vibrational beings. And it is their children who are really going to take a hold of this planet, really going to start to listen to the planet as the life form it is, and really release the planet to do what the planet wants to do. They will no longer try to own it or try to control it or change it. They will seek to live in harmony with Gaia, the living planet who also is a spiritual being, who also is ascending in a higher-vibrational way.

When you transform from life on Earth, then it is our time to come back down from the higher-vibrational realm of spirit. You will be "as above," and "so below" becomes us. When we are in the physical form, we want to have a good connection with the spirit realm. We want it to be natural. We want it to be close so that when we are on the planet talking to you in the spirit realm, we want you to respond easily.

We know it is going to be challenging when we are back on the planet. There will be messes to clean up. Yes, it is getting better, but it is going to be hard work. There is a deconstruction going on, and the old, dogmatic energy is holding on and trying to pull things back.

Dualistic fundamentalism is working really hard to restructure you so that you fit into an old box, and you do not want to go there, do you? No, because you are spiritually minded, and you cannot put spirit into a box no matter how hard you try.

You are already a mature spiritual being, currently on the planet in a physical form. All you need to do is get off the planet to again act fully in a spiritual way.

If you are acting in love and joy and peace, then you are already walking with us and we with you, together as it has always been. As it will always be.

Conclusions

As LIFE EVOLVES, will there be an end to death? This is sort of the point. There is no death. There are only stages of transformation. You do not mourn the fact that you are no longer a toddler. You do not mourn the fact that you are no longer going through puberty. Why, then, would you mourn the fact that you are no longer human? These are stages of a repeating cycle.

When loved ones pass, you might feel their force at a higher vibration. Their vibrations, their paths, now shift and change. They are not your simply your guides. They are not just your angels. They are still your friends, your companions. So we direct you to think in those terms, spiritual companions, not merely guides or angels. You guide each other, and we have said these things before.

Your associations with your spirit companions, your association with those who have passed from this life, this earthly realm, help you to raise your vibration and help you to have a truer vision of what it will be like when you yourself take that step from gravity into the realm of spirit.

As often happens on earth, your spiritual companions may change. They change based on their needs as much as yours, so be aware of that. There are many responsibilities at whatever level life exists. The simpler the life, the lower the vibration and the less the responsibility, until sometimes it is just a matter of being still so that other things can grow. If perhaps things around you are still, it is so that you can grow. Stillness is an aspect of the creative energies of the universe.

Appreciation is also an aspect of the creative energies of the universe. When we say, "appreciate," what we want to indicate is for you to look at things as they truly are and understand their value.

Be in gratitude for everything that is around you. Be grateful for those who have been with you. In this way, as your life transforms, it becomes easier. You will find that your energy is in cooperation with the rest of the universe, for Source is grateful.

There is power within you. Create a new path of conclusion for earthly life. It is not a stopping of life. It is a transition of life. Take joy in a life well lived. Love those who have brought you your purifying lessons. Be at peace when the moment of transference comes.

Jeff Michaels has agreed to be the voice for Onereon: a warm, insightful, and compassionate "human resource" group, here to assist us to navigate the current waves of energy.

Onereon believes in us and our ability to grow and evolve. Much of what they say is indicative of the future of humanity and the vitality of the planetary system of which we are a part.

www.OnereonChannels.com

www.ingramcontent.com/pod-product-compliance
Lightning Source LLC
Chambersburg PA
CBHW072047040426
42447CB00012BB/3057